Printed in the USA

# INFJ:
# The Lives of 13 Great INFJ's

By Leanne Silva

# Contents

# Great INFJs

INFJs are a rare breed, and it's a shame because they are capable of so much! Then again, if there were more INFJs in the world, they might not seem quite as special and would end up even less appreciated than they already are. Some of the greatest people who have lived and done good works in this world were INFJs, including writers, civil leaders, and even acclaimed actors, so if you are an INFJ, you are in good company. If you know someone who is an INFJ or you suspect he or she might be, here is a quick run-down of the unique characteristics that make this personality type who they are.

Introverts are often misunderstood because while many of them are shy and retiring, plenty of them can be outgoing and outspoken! It's just that after they have their moment in the spotlight, they need to step away and be at peace, have time to collect their thoughts, and recharge their batteries. INFJs have the capacity to be leaders of entire nations, but they need their "me time" all the same, and many go to great lengths to ensure that they schedule those essential moments into their daily lives. Often, INFJs use those quiet, contemplative periods for some artistic endeavor, like writing or reading.

Intuitives are the dreamers who hope for a better tomorrow. While Thinking Intuitives tend to wonder, "What can I invent? How can I make this machine work better?" Feeling Intuitives like INFJs want to engender greater social harmony and better interpersonal relationships. To their thinking, if people can get along better, then the future will be much brighter. Intuitives like INFJs also tend to look at the big picture, rather than focus on smaller details, and they are comfortable thinking about abstract ideas and theoretical situations.

Feeling types are the do-gooders who often place the emotional needs of others before their own. Their focus is on how word and action makes others feel, and while making decisions based on a feeling can land them in trouble at times (for instance, acting on a rush of emotion rather than logically thinking through a problem can be dangerous), their hearts are almost always in the right place. Their compassion and empathy make them relatable and immediately likable.

Judging personalities have the innate ambition and drive to get things done in a timely and responsible manner. Perceivers tend to take their own meandering paths when it comes to their pursuits, both in their careers and personal lives, but Judging types are much more committed; their actions have a feeling of agency to them, which is why INFJs are so subtly formidable — they are underdogs, the secret weapons employed by those who recognize their strength and ambition.

Here are 13 great examples of some famous INFJs who have helped shape the course of history.

# 1. Geoffrey Chaucer

His Introvert Advantage: Geoffrey Chaucer was many things: a poet, a philosopher, and a diplomat, but he was, above all, a wit, and he had the ability to see things with his keen observer's eye. He might have had a silvery tongue (as anyone employed on overseas missions for the king must), but from the works he left us, it is obvious that, like an Introvert, he preferred to sit back and watch, take everything in, and consider, rather than jump into the action and put himself at the front. That he wrote at all is not necessarily an indication that he was an Introvert (as it never is), but the sheer volume of the works that Chaucer produced indicates that he was comfortable being closeted away for long periods of time, bent over his manuscripts. Chaucer held many different positions over his lifetime, working in quite a variety of fields, and it is suggested that he modeled many of his characters (especially those in *The Canterbury Tales*) after the people he met, a task that takes no small amount of time or concentration, especially when the characters are so brilliantly satirized.

His Intuitive Advantage: Like many Intuitives, Chaucer was gifted with languages, and he would not have been chosen for diplomatic ventures had he not been fluent in French, the standard language of the courts of Europe. Only those with an elite grasp of the language would be able to undertake translation work, as Chaucer did. While he worked at the court, there can be no doubt that he was kept busy, as Medieval kingdoms and politics were highly complex and inordinately inefficient, and he was in charge of overseeing the king's building projects for a time. Yet it is while he held this post that scholars attribute many of his writings, proving that Geoffrey Chaucer had that undeniable impulse to create and to imagine, two traits that every Intuitive can relate to. One can easily imagine him with his public face on, energetic and practical, then retiring to his chambers with candles all around him, gaining quiet energy as he made his words come to life, a great Prometheus at his forge, the urge to write as strong as the need to breathe.

His Feeling Advantage: Though it is disputed, historians and scholars generally agree that Chaucer's *The Book of the Duchess* was composed to commemorate the death of Blanche of Lancaster, the wife of John of Gaunt (one of the younger sons of the illustrious Edward III). Though she was a great heiress and the marriage was arranged, it appears to have been a happy one, and the two produced 10 children (7 of whom survived infancy). She died very young, only about 22 or 23, and there are indications that, though Gaunt married twice more after her death, he sincerely mourned her passing. Historians have suggested that *The Book of the Duchess*, which describes the mourning of a knight for his lady "White" (Blanche being a French-derived word for white), is certainly meant to honor her, perhaps for one of the special anniversary commemorations that Gaunt held each year, but it was also meant to coax this prince out of his grave sadness. A Feeling Chaucer seems to be suggesting that her death was indeed very tragic, but as even the lowliest peasant must do, so must a prince of England find the will to carry on.

His Judging Advantage: In a way, if it weren't for Chaucer's industriousness around the court, signs of his Judging nature, we would know significantly less about the author who left us the richly hilarious work, *The Canterbury Tales*. Since very few people from this time left any of their own written accounts of their lives (blogging hadn't quite taken off yet), we must rely on the legal and court documents which detail the activities of the king and courtiers. Thankfully, Chaucer was part of the busy environment, starting as a squire and working his way up to more illustrious positions — not bad for a kid whose family sold wine. That he was able to do so is an indication of both his intelligence and his ambition; one gets the sense that this was a guy who aimed high and took his chance when it was presented. Making tough decisions that turn out to be great decisions is something that successful Judging types do, and Chaucer is a fine example of that. Despite the fact that he lived through considerable political upheaval — the unfortunate reign of Richard II, who was deposed by his cousin, Henry IV — his ability to do the work that was asked of him with a sense of urgency and responsibility stood him in good stead and he never lost footing while the hands of government changed.

# 2. Gillian Anderson

Her Introvert Advantage: Gillian Anderson had rather inconspicuous beginnings. She was born into a family that moved to Puerto Rico from Chicago when she was only 15 months old, then moved on to England when she was about two. At the age of 11, Anderson returned with her family to the United States, where the kids of Grand Rapids, Michigan, picked her on for her English accent, so she quickly modified her speech to sound more American. She describes herself as a punk in her teen years, one of the few kids, let alone girls, who wore her hair in a Mohawk and donned a nose ring, and as the outside world stared, she withdrew further into herself, using isolation as armor. Her Introversion was further fostered by the claustrophobic work schedule she maintained while on set for *The X-Files*, her break-out TV show; she met her first husband and had a baby, and when she wasn't working, which wasn't often, she clung to those quiet, domestic moments where there was no one talking at her and she could just be, without distractions, and those are the types of Introverted moments that sustained her through nine years of the show.

Her Intuitive Advantage: When she was 24 and just starting *The X-Files*, Gillian Anderson had no clear picture of her future; she got word that she had nabbed the part on the day her last unemployment check arrived, so she was just happy to have a job and some income. Yet as her success grew more assured, she blossomed as an actress and began to take on a variety of different roles, seeing herself as more than just a TV FBI agent. One gets the sense that her Intuitive aspect grew and matured as she did, both in her years and in confidence. Despite her success, Gillian maintains her "weirdness," a clear indication that her creative juices are still flowing, and her desire to make sense out of chaos — as words on a page inevitably are, until we inject meaning and nuance into them — continues more powerfully than it has before. As an actress who has taken on a wealth of roles, from a *belle époque* beauty in *The House of*

*Mirth* to the melodramatic Blanche DuBois in *A Streetcar Named Desire*, Gillian ably uses her body to interpret and emote.

Her Feeling Advantage: While actors and actresses clearly rely on the impetus of their own emotions, as well as those of their audience, to produce effective work, Gillian Anderson is also a devoted humanitarian who uses her celebrity to effect positive change in the world around her. Her activism is wide and varied, from speaking on behalf of the Neurofibromatosis Network (which is particularly dear to her heart because her brother was diagnosed with it and then died when he was only 31 years old), to making much of her support of PETA. She has been aligned with the LGBT community for years, and has also spoken out in favor of international women's rights. In her personal life Gillian Anderson has shown a strong desire to love and be loved, and she seeks out committed relationships; for her first child, she felt such a protective, motherly concern that she refused to let her daughter be photographed until the child was 7 years old.

Her Judging Advantage: Gillian Anderson has said that she considers herself to be controlling, but my, how far that "controlling" Judging nature has taken her. Though in her younger years she might have been considered more of a Perceiving type, age and maturity have done their work, and she is now a reliable and committed actress. Her lengthy body of work, as well as her numerous nominations (with a few impressive awards!), is a fine example of how ambitious and decisive this actress can be when it comes to choosing roles that will challenge her and offer her the opportunity to show range — range that extends far beyond the skeptical, tight-lipped Dana Scully. Though many writers can show the traits of a Perceiving type, Gillian Anderson has shown a surprising aptitude for the written word; it has been 15 years, and she is still doggedly adapting a novel about the children of a Holocaust survivor into a screenplay, which she also intends to one day direct. Whereas Perceivers would have given up and moved onto something else after 15 days or 15 weeks, this is only proof that Gillian Anderson wants to see things finished, and finished the right way.

# 3. Cate Blanchett

Her Introvert Advantage: When one of her directors commented, "She's a private person," he could not have described Cate Blanchett better. This screen siren, who is bound to remind us all of the icon from the Golden Age of Hollywood, has scooped up numerous awards (it's really not an award season unless she is nominated for something) and has earned a reputation for being one of the most brilliant actresses on the planet; yet aside from glossy magazine covers, you don't realize she's there until another one of her fabulous movies comes out. This is because Cate is essentially an Introvert, and though she can float down the red carpet looking like a goddess and call out a fashion show for blatant sexism ("Do you do that to the guys?" she asked, as the camera swept from her ankles upward), it is obvious that her need for privacy and isolation, far away from the paparazzi and the crowds of screaming fans, is a priority, both for herself and for her entire family, which consists of her husband, three boys, and one girl.

Her Intuitive Advantage: Truly, no one dazzles on screen the way Cate Blanchett does, and her ability to interpret lines and turn them into the utterings of real people who have real feelings and real motivations is astounding. This is particularly obvious in her range, as she has played a powerful elf from Middle Earth, Queen Elizabeth I, a narcissistic socialite who is suddenly stricken with hard financial times, a lost schoolteacher who commits adultery with a student...and the list goes on and on, and it's not just that she takes on these roles, but that her Intuitive aspect is so fine-tuned that she makes each and every one of them come utterly alive, to the point where you forget that you are watching an actress at her craft. Her vision for the arts is also apparent, as she served with her husband as co-CEO and artistic director for the Sydney Theater Company, a more administrative role that nonetheless required her to look ahead to the future of theater in Australia and make decisions about where the company was heading.

Her Feeling Advantage: Cate has been married since 1997, and it is interesting that she regards her husband as one of the few people she can discuss work with; she considers him to be the font of constructive criticism. Feeling types can have a very difficult time taking critique, but it is obvious that this emotional and professional woman found someone whose emotion and professionalism matched hers. Her compassion for the less fortunate was brought to light more tellingly in 2015, when it was confirmed that she and her husband, who already had three boys, decided to adopt a little girl. Cate cited the need to get children out of foster homes and into permanent families as part of her husband's and her desire to adopt, displaying immense empathy for the millions of children stuck in the foster care system. She has also shown support for causes that aim to improve the environment and provide clean drinking water to people have little-to-no access, and she has been an outspoken proponent for gender equality both around the world and in the arts.

Her Judging Advantage: One gets the distinct impression that in Hollywood there are a few different types of actors, and that Cate Blanchett belongs in the group with those who choose to behave with class, style, and graciousness. If she had gone into a professional career, she would be at the top of the company, the CEO — such are her administrative gifts and her ability to pay attention to details — but as an actress, she relays her stardom into projects that are greater than herself and require serious commitments of time and responsibility. Then there is her family life, which is so indicative of her Judging personality. She married her husband in 1997, and their only major blips have involved health issues, not fidelity problems. They have three boys, and adopted a little girl in 2015, and they moved back to their native Australia to be closer to family and have a deeper sense of connection with the country from which they came. None of this has had any impact on Cate's acting career, and indeed it seems as though her steady, secure private life has been an anchor for her glamorous, international acting career.

# 4. Nelson Mandela

His Introvert Advantage: Just because Introverts tend to be quieter, happier in the background, and less sociable than their Extraverted counterparts, we might assume that they are less capable of managing big matters and effecting great change. This is a deeply flawed logic that is refuted by Nelson Mandela, the first South African president and one of the most influential and courageous men to have walked the planet. His Introversion has been decided by the man himself, who described his own personality as "serious" and "observant," two traits that get thrown at Introverts quite a bit. Yet his Introversion opened the door to serious and intelligent political thought and deep introspection about who he was as a man and what he hoped to achieve. He was deeply influenced by his roots in the tribal community where he was raised, where the king would only speak after everyone else had spoken; throughout the gatherings, the man in charge did not lead the discussions, but instead let all else have their say, and as they talked and argued, he observed them — what they were saying, how they said it, and what was the measure of each man.

His Intuitive Advantage: It is hard to imagine that after 27 years in prison Nelson Mandela kept his dreams alive, but he did; his Intuitive nature did not simply up and vanish because of the conditions of his surroundings. He continued his journey toward what he knew would be a better tomorrow, even in his prison, even after contracting tuberculosis. He was able to complete a law degree remotely through the University of South Africa, and he worked in secret on an autobiography (which would be published after his release, in the year he became president). Is this the behavior of a man who has given up all hope of a future? Are these the actions of a man who has resigned himself and his country to a system of legal racism? It most certainly is not, and though Mandela's Intuitive aspect must have struggled throughout the years of incarceration to keep hope alive, it did prevail, so that when he was released, the first thing he did was urge foreign powers to continue their pressure on the South

African government (which they had been doing in large part to urge the release of Mandela).

His Feeling Advantage: Called "Tata" or "father," Mandela is revered in South Africa as the father of the country. While he wanted to see blacks raised up to the same level as whites, he hoped to achieve this as peacefully as possible during his time as president, which is notable for its dismantling of apartheid. It seems that every moment he spent in jail, he was thinking about the welfare of the people who would eventually elect him to the highest position in the land. He once declared himself prepared to die for his ideals — he was therefore prepared to die for the idea that everyone should be treated equally and racism should not be tolerated, let alone sanctioned by the state. Compassion for people he did not know and had never met was one of the defining traits of Nelson Mandela, as it is one of the aspects of the Feeling function.

His Judging Advantage: INFJs are like the administrative, more responsible siblings to INFPs, and Mandela exemplified all that a committed, loyal, and reliable man should be. He not only stood up for his ideals, but he was also willing to put in the legwork necessary to see them brought to action, no matter how hard the current rushed in the other direction. That he refused release from his prison in exchange for desisting from armed opposition (he came to the conclusion reluctantly, after years of peaceful protest, that armed opposition was the only way to get his government to implement change), staying loyal to his beliefs, and to the trust that others had placed in him, without a moment's hesitation. Then he led the way for his country, shouldering the immense responsibility of running an entire nation that was still badly bruised from decades of hate and fearmongering, and he did it with humanity, warmth, and a strong sense of moral right.

# 5. Martin Luther King, Jr.

His Introvert Advantage: It might seem surprising that one of the most charismatic and moving public speakers to have ever lived was also an Introvert, but there is no denying that Martin Luther King, Jr. did was what necessary — indeed, what moved him in his heart — for the good of social change, yet he remained a private individual who kept his friends close and his family closer. A precocious student, once King applied himself to his studies, he showed immense promise as a scholar, entering college at the age of 15, graduating by 18, and earning his doctoral degree before he was 25. While he was phenomenally intelligent, it speaks to his gifts as an Introvert — gifts of observation and contemplation — that he was able to accelerate his studies at such a speed. Then there was his ability not just to lead, but also to listen — as an observer in a world that was changing fast, King opened his ears like an Introvert and heard people's suggestions and opinions.

His Intuitive Advantage: "I have a dream," King intoned in his most famous speech, and he could very well have followed that up with, "for I am an Intuitive" (but thankfully he didn't!). His Intuitive aspect shows in the work that he did and the vision that he strived for his entire life — the equality of all men and women in the world, regardless of skin color. There is no telling why some people can participate half heartedly in a cause while others make it their sole reason for drawing breath, but King was most certainly in the latter group, and he held onto his goal and his hope for a better tomorrow — indeed, he clung to it with the ferocity of a man thrown overboard with only a lifesaver. He was arrested 29 times for his willingness to be identified as part of the Civil Rights Movement, and his speech at the 1963 March on Washington electrified the entire nation with its impassioned call for a country in which all stood on equal footing.

His Feeling Advantage: One of King's most astounding traits was the lengths to which he was prepared to go so that all of his brothers and sisters in love and unity could be part of a world which welcomed them equally — not segregated them. King lived out his adult life in the service of others, yet there is an equally fascinating Feeling personality who emerges out of what we know to be evidence that he participated in extramarital affairs. King was not a saint; he was a man as human and as flawed as any of us, and his deeply emotional behavior is an indication of how he could act without logic at times. Yet it in no way diminishes his powerful and positive influence on the course of American history; if anything, it makes him even more relatable to the rest of us "regular" people who feel as though we are too flawed to do good.

His Judging Advantage: King's Judging aspect seemed to articulate itself when he was a junior at Morehouse College and still just a teenager. Despite his youth, King's spiritual growth helped him mature and become the committed, devoted man and civil leader he would blossom into in his 20s and 30s. His thoughtful and contemplative nature allowed him to more fully articulate his feelings and opinions when it came to the forward motion of the Civil Rights Movement, but his Judging aspect imbued him with the extraordinary ambition and drive to see his ideals through to completion. Though he lived to see successes for his movement, there is no doubt that he was capable of much more, and were it not for his tragic assassination in 1968, America might be an even greater bastion of equality.

# 6. Mother Teresa

Her Introvert Advantage: Aside from all the good things that Mother Teresa did for people throughout her long life, one of her most significant contributions to this world was that she listened to people. Introverts have a bad rap for being shy or afraid to speak up, and they are sometimes underappreciated for their lack of spoken words. Yet just because Introverts aren't speaking, it doesn't automatically follow that they are not communicating. Many beautiful quotes have been attributed to Mother Teresa, but she was first and foremost an observer and a listener, a woman who preferred that her speech and her needs take a backseat to service for others and for her God. The world is a much better place because Mother Teresa chose to look around herself in the Introverted fashion and witness the poverty, illness, and social injustice that needed fixing.

Her Intuitive Advantage: Only a woman with such tremendous insight and hope for the future could place the rest of her life in the hands of the Catholic Church at the age of 18. That is precisely what Mother Teresa did, making her way toward Ireland (from her home in Albania) to join a religious order in Dublin, where she could learn English and then be sent as a missionary to India. Mother Teresa's belief — instilled in her from the time she was very young by her charitable mother — that service to others was the highest calling and the best way to change the world around her and lift people out of their poverty manifested itself in a religious calling, to which she remained faithful her entire life. Her idealistic hopes that she could effect change never left her, and indeed, it seemed to grow stronger as she matured.

Her Feeling Advantage: Mother Teresa was, in a way, the living embodiment of the Feeling aspect. Her every action from the time she was 18 was in service to others. With her incredible stores of compassion and empathy, she felt deeply the pain and suffering that others endured. While her own upbringing was not one of lavish wealth, she recognized how lucky she had been to receive a formal education, and it was soon after she arrived in India that she saw the truest and most desperate forms of poverty. Never one to let evil or injustice stand, she threw herself into her charitable works, learning Bengali and Hindu so that she could fluently communicate with the children of the Indian villages, eventually moving into the slums of Calcutta to aid the poor who lived and died there — people forgotten by everyone else, but not by Mother Teresa, who made it her life's mission to improve their quality of life.

Her Judging Advantage: It is interesting to note that when Christ spoke to Mother Teresa and told her to change her plans from teaching to simply "helping the poor," He didn't leave her with anything more concrete than that. It was this remarkable woman who transformed His word into the vast network of charitable organizations that became an international source of refuge and hope for the world's poor. She helped to establish schools, hospitals, orphanages, and shelters all around the world, and when AIDS became a new, terrifying epidemic the world over, she threw herself into the care of those who contracted and suffered with the disease. She did this with the devotion, commitment, and sense of responsibility that makes all Judging types capable of reaching out to others — from a place of vision and a sense of moral right — to better our little planet.

# 7. Mahatma Gandhi

His Introvert Advantage: In a way, Mahatma Gandhi was subjected to a life of introversion whether he liked it or not — he frequently spent long periods of time away from his family and conversed with friends by mail. But the Father of India was deeply Introverted in his own way, an observant individual who absorbed experiences and sights and then reflected on them, made sense of them, and gathered strength and energy in the process of articulating his thoughts and opinions. He found himself in the limelight on many occasions, but he never sought it for any reason other than to bring attention to his goals, preferring to do all that he could for his causes without thrusting himself forward for acclaim. He was a man who valued learning for its own sake, and he often immersed himself in the cultures of the people around whom he lived, and was willing to stop and hear out the opinions and philosophies of others.

His Intuitive Advantage: Though Gandhi urged others to act in the present and not worry about the future, he himself was quite concerned about the future for the sake of the people he represented. In his 21 years in South Africa, where he experienced, first hand, the racism and classism that plagued the country and particularly took aim at Indians who lived there, he saw even worse examples of injustice in the impoverished and beaten-down people who struggled to get through every day. When he finally returned to his native India, he took aim at the British government that had occupied India as part of its empire. With a great sense of destiny for the Indian people, he worked tirelessly to gain Indian independence from Britain, as well as to level the playing field for all people, and gain more equal rights for women.

His Feeling Advantage: Though Gandhi was trained as a lawyer and obviously had a well-developed Thinking aspect that allowed him to act with thoughtful and logical analysis, his Feeling aspect provided the impetus to put those legal skills into practice for the greater good. Certainly his sharp intelligence and keen understanding of legal matters were a boon when he was facing off against an empire, but without his Feeling aspect, he might not have felt compelled to face off against anyone to begin with. For Gandhi, the fight was about justness, freedom and autonomy. Too long had his country been subjected to the rule of a foreign power that misused and abused the Indian people, and Gandhi translated his immense distaste for the British Empire's tyrannical rule into the tireless campaign for independence that was called "Quit India". Throughout his life and all of his social and political activities, he strongly advocated for non-violent protest because, as he put it, "An eye for an eye would soon make the whole world blind."

His Judging Advantage: Gandhi's magnificent ability to galvanize and to attain progress was not just because of his idealism. Aside from being well educated, he was thoughtful about how to approach each campaign and he displayed a talent for being a good organizer of both people and action. He was also incredibly disciplined, living simply, eating no meat, and sometimes eating nothing for weeks so that his fasts could have a more profound influence on the people he opposed. And he was never once heard to complain or whine; he did it all willingly, happily even, because once he committed himself to a cause, he was there to stay, present in mind, body, and spirit. He had the typical Judging patience, the ability to play the long game, and he never showed resentment for the fact that results couldn't be achieved any faster than they were. Moreover, as a parent does for his child, Gandhi never gave up on his people. No wonder they called him "father"!

# 8. Eleanor Roosevelt

Her Introvert Advantage: Eleanor Roosevelt was born into a wealthy and recognizable family — her uncle, Teddy, gave her away at her wedding while he was sitting president — yet her childhood was as distant and unhappy as one could imagine. Naturally, a cold childhood does not an Introvert make, but it did leave this eventual First Lady with the impression that she could not rely on others for happiness, and if she wanted to get anything done in the face of opposition, she would have to summon her courage and do it, naysayers be damned. Though she was well liked and charmingly outspoken, Eleanor nonetheless kept close to herself, ensuring that her private life and inner emotions stayed private — and for good reason. Letters written between Eleanor and a Washington, D.C., journalist named Lorena Hickok hint strongly at a lesbian relationship; what would be scandalous today would have been unspeakably damaging to her and her husband's reputations back then.

Her Intuitive Advantage: When Franklin Delano Roosevelt came home from a long trip, his wife Eleanor did the wifely thing: she put his tired bones to bed and then set about unpacking his luggage. What she found in his suitcase changed the tenor of their relationship as we know it. Letters that proved he was in love with a younger woman were contained therein, but instead of folding with misery under the discovery, Eleanor took advantage of her position of power (a gentle threat of divorce was enough to make him come to his senses) and ferried his marital failings into her political future. This was in 1918, and by the time FDR had achieved the heights of his ambitions — becoming president — his First Lady had an equally ambitious vision for what her position in the White House would encompass. She had gone from shrinking violet under her mother-in-law's iron rule to independent and visionary political and social activist with a voice that was all her own.

Her Feeling Advantage: Eleanor had the great fortune to be married to a man who, once he realized what an asset she was, encouraged and supported her political and social activities while he was president. In turn, the country was made a better place because Eleanor worked with impressive ambition to improve the situation of America's women and children, to bring about greater civil justice for blacks, to advocate on behalf of the poor and to show her support for the troops during World War II. On the one hand, it greatly enhanced her own prestige and the public support of her husband, but on the other, this was a genuinely independent-thinking woman who wanted to use her position of great importance — and her unique access to the most powerful man in the world — to help others less fortunate. With her great Intuitive aspect paired with her Feeling function, Eleanor Roosevelt realized that by strengthening the weak, the entire country grew stronger as a whole.

Her Judging Advantage: With her keen political mind and no-nonsense attitude, First Lady Eleanor Roosevelt exemplified the virtues of the Judging type. She planned and put into action many different initiatives, programs and personal ventures, whether it was traveling to meet and speak with the poor and hear their stories, making public speaking engagements so that people could come out and see their First Lady (the fees almost all went to charity), or writing a syndicated newspaper column called "My Day" — which gave her readers the unprecedented feeling that she was right there with them, offering her ideas and thoughts. She was organized, she was galvanized and, perhaps surprisingly, after discovering her husband's letters from another woman, she was a devoted wife to her polio-stricken husband, choosing to move past the hurt and throw her focus and ambition into working with him to carve out a better, more just America.

# 9. Carl Jung

His Introvert Advantage: Carl Jung, one of the pioneers of modern psychiatry and the man who formed the personality theory upon which Isabel Briggs Myers based the MBTI system, was an obvious Introvert from a very young age. Socially awkward and not good at making friends, he even started faking illness in order to stay home from school and further isolate himself from others. Though in childhood this was rather unfortunate (as it is for lots of Introverts), as an adult it manifested itself in much more constructive ways, making Jung noticeably serious, contemplative, observant, and willing to invest hours into involved, deep discussions with close associates (like Freud), in readings of lengthy and complex tomes for greater understanding of his field, and in writing his own books, which he published right up to his death.

His Intuitive Advantage: Intuitives don't mind getting their hands dirty with the less-than-concrete — unlike Sensing types, hard facts are less desirable than possibilities and theories, and Jung played around with this perspective throughout his entire career. Intuitives are known as interpreters, and while some may use this to their advantage and acquire a new language (or two), Jung was interested in dream interpretation — what our subconscious is telling us while we sleep. But he was also a proponent of art therapy, using the creation of art to alleviate stress and depression and to explore the hidden depths of an individual. He himself turned to art for this reason, showing the Intuitive impulse for creativity as a means to express something that cannot be put into words. Ultimately, Jung provided an innovative way of looking at psychology, introducing or expanding on ideas that might not receive the attention they do today if he had not paved the way.

His Feeling Advantage: There has been some debate over whether or not Carl Jung was an INFJ. There is some sentiment that he might have been an INTJ, the master architect. While it's true that Jung undertook no great charitable words and his passions were rather ordinary, his emphasis on the spiritual and metaphysical make a strong argument for his being a Feeling type rather than a Thinking type. For instance, rather than advocate a strict dietary regimen or exercise schedule, Jung suggested that one of the ways alcoholics cope with abstaining is through spirituality. He was personally interested in many different types of religions and religious philosophies, and he theorized that only through spirituality could an individual be truly happy. That he was concerned at all with happiness — over, say, usefulness or efficiency — indicates Jung's preference for Feeling (although he clearly had a well-defined Thinking aspect that was used to great effect).

His Judging Advantage: Carl Jung was a social scientist, and as a successful professional whose work has withstood many decades without any large-scale debunking (scientists will always squabble and debate, but there is no denying his influence), he has proven to be detail oriented and ambitious about his life's work. His writing is so full of nuance and complexity that it would be hard to believe a Perceiving type could dedicate such a large part of his life to committing all of these ideas to paper, let alone keep up the relentless correspondence that Jung did with the great thinkers of his day. Jung met life with a seriousness that is both Introverted and Judging, showing a solitary dedication for a field that he didn't even think about entering when he first matriculated at university, but that captivated him after he discovered its dual emphasis on both body and mind.

# 10. Florence Nightingale

Her Introvert Advantage: Insightful and serene even in the face of the bloodiest chaos, Florence Nightingale in her youth was described as being awkward in social situations and, like a true Introvert, she loathed being the center of attention, something that must have vexed her mother, who fancied herself a socialite. A graceful youth, Florence was a lovely young woman, but despite her physical charms she preferred not to thrust herself forward and seek the limelight. Indeed, her attention from the start was captured by the sick and the impoverished, and she knew from a young age what she wanted to do with her life. Like many an Introvert, Florence — who was named after the city in Italy where she was born to wealthy, upper-class parents — held her dreams close and only showed her hand when it was absolutely necessary. Then, she clung to her desires with a stubbornness that shocked her parents, who forbade her from pursuing a career — scandalous in the first place — in nursing, of all practices.

Her Intuitive Advantage: Nursing is like a religious calling: it is a vocation, and it is not to be taken lightly. One must feel it deep down inside one's very being, from a place that cannot be described or articulated. This is what Florence felt as a child who helped to care for the sick and poor people near her ancestral home in England. It was a feeling beyond fact or evidence, and it was likely that her Intuitive aspect is what made sense of the urge and gave her the ability to understand what her path in life must be. Florence displayed other apparent Intuitive traits as well, such as her gift for languages — she studied French, Italian and German, in addition to her native English. Her writing shows a flair for description, melding her knowledge of classical literature with her own bright, thirsty mind. And though she was a Victorian woman, born into a wealthy family that expected her to marry and produce children, Florence always had that Intuitive sense that she was destined for much more.

Her Feeling Advantage: There are few people in this world who have done as much as Florence Nightingale to help our sick and our poor, and it all stems from her natural compassion and empathy toward people who were born with much, much less than she. Sometimes "causes" can be fashionable, such as the modern-day "green" movement and the organics sections that have cropped up in all of our supermarkets, but that most certainly was not the case in the 19th century. While caring for the poor on a superficial level was considered good breeding by a lady of means (distributing alms, sewing linens, and even visiting sick villagers), actually tending to them as a career, rather than as an item on one's to-do list, was not a stylish trend, and Florence's Feeling aspect was therefore sincere, an innate part of who she was and the driving force behind the actions that would lead her to become the beloved Lady of the Lamp, and perhaps the most famous nurse who ever lived.

Her Judging Advantage: Florence Nightingale wasn't just a nurse — she utterly changed and redefined the concept of nursing as a career. This is where her Judging aspect is most obvious; when she was sent to administer care to the soldiers of the Crimean War, while acting as manager of the corps of nurses, she managed to turn around the horrific conditions the women discovered when they arrived at Istanbul. Her first course of action was to effectively shame the British government, by way of a public letter to the London Times, into providing better facilities and medical equipment for the wounded and sick. Thereafter, her committed and continuous advocacy on behalf of the soldiers in Crimea helped to reduce the death rate to 1/10th of what it had been before she arrived. And she didn't stop there; for the rest of her life, Florence Nightingale was a proponent for an organized, trained nursing system, and her book, *Notes on Nursing*, which was culled from her experiences and insights, is still read by new nursing students today.

# 11. Jimmy Carter

His Introvert Advantage: One might think that in order to be the leader of the free world, an Extraverted personality is an absolute necessity. One might think wrong. Look at Jimmy Carter, the 39th president of the United States, and an Introvert through and through. He is actually an exemplary Introvert, as he embodies the true spirit of the aspect. He is capable without being flashy, commanding but not overwhelming or "in your face," and an able communicator thanks to his introspective nature, which keeps him from blurting out the first thing that crosses his mind. While he has been described as shy, there is no doubting that when the matter at hand is one that has his full attention, he can be as forceful and purposeful as any Extravert, if not more so because he has taken the time to thoroughly consider the matter before resting on a decision.

His Intuitive Advantage: Like many great men, Jimmy Carter had an idea of how the country should be. But before he took on Washington, he worked hard as governor in his own state of Georgia, improving the efficiency of the government there and working to expand the opportunities for poor people and people of color. He showed incredible vision in all of his changes, especially in a state deeply entrenched in the South, where the vestiges of the "Gone with the Wind" era were still visible. He took his dreams and his ideals to the White House in 1977, and there he added two of the most important departments to our nation's future: the Department of Education and the Department of Energy. He was deeply forward thinking, Intuitive in his belief — far ahead of his time — that the way to a better tomorrow in America was through the education of its young people and the proper harnessing and usage of energies.

His Feeling Advantage: Carter had a special reason to champion the causes of the poor in America: when his family farm fell on hard times after the death of his father, he and his wife, and their family, were forced to rely on government-subsidized housing. Though he was a humble man to begin with, this experience gave him a personal taste of what life was like for the impoverished, and he never forgot that. His governance and presidency were filled with nods specifically to African Americans, poor people, and others who suffered from oppression. In his post-presidential years, Carter has been a champion of human rights all around the globe, and in 2002 this undeniably Feeling man won the Nobel Peace Prize for his tireless work in finding peaceable solutions to the crises that inflict unspeakable horrors on people all around the globe.

His Judging Advantage: Carter has always funneled his energies through his Judging aspect, so that when he sets out to do something, he does it with great thoughtfulness, attention to detail, and organization, so that his endeavors are less likely to fail from the outset. His Judging aspect is, at times, what gives him such steely ambition and unwillingness to back down from the things he truly believes in. Interestingly enough, the Judging part of his personality can be seen in his handling of the gubernatorial race in Georgia in the 1970. Here, he played the long game, displaying the patience that only a Judging type can summon. To woo voters, he gave the appearance of dropping his civil rights platform entirely, a strategy that must have been excruciating; yet once he won, he resumed his previous efforts on behalf of the African-American population, much to the consternation of the pro-segregation voters he won.

# 12. Mary Wollstonecraft

Her Introvert Advantage: Brilliantly intellectual and astonishingly passionate, Mary Wollstonecraft is perhaps best known for birthing the novelist who penned *Frankenstein*, Mary Wollstonecraft Shelley, yet she was an entirely gifted and forward-thinking woman in her own right. Throughout her life, she formed intense attachments with her friends, focusing much of her attention on them (in one instance, even leaving the school she had founded to help nurse a woman in Lisbon, Portugal). Though she was good company, her preference for the inner world inside her mind was obvious — she was a prolific writer, both professionally as an author and personally, as a diarist. In a way, she had to turn inward because the ideas that she had were so scandalous that when her widower published her biography, her reputation was blackened for a century.

Her Intuitive Advantage: Intuitives live in a world beyond the physical: a mental, intellectual, and emotional plane where ideas reign supreme. Unorthodox and unconventional Mary Wollstonecraft might not have outwardly defied the norms of 18th-century England, but her mind was practically swarming with ideas that could have gotten her imprisoned. Though she married and produced children like a good Georgian woman should, inside she was fiery, open-minded, and untraditional. Her creative impulses compelled her to write, and though she only did so for a brief time (she died when she was just 38 years old), her work reveals the innermost thoughts of a woman trapped by time and space, but yearning for a more perfect tomorrow. That tomorrow entailed a world where men and women lived side by side in equality; she blamed the dominant patriarchal society for making women weak when, if they were free, they could become just as strong and smart as any man.

Her Feeling Advantage: Mary grew up in a tumultuous household, with a father who wasted his money on doomed ventures and then drank himself into a rage, beating Mary's mother. Though her work describes a keen logic, it is experiences like these — raw, emotional — that ultimately made it impossible for her not to take up the pen and ink and put her incredibly rebellious thoughts to paper. She imagined a world where no little girl would have to sleep across the doorway of her mother's bedroom to protect her from an inebriated, violent father; she wrote so that, in her dream of dreams, her words might inspire a movement that would bring about a society where a wife who left her husband would not be shunned by society and forced to work in the only conditions afforded to women who deserted — soul-crushing labor in extreme poverty.

Her Judging Advantage: Though she spent a lot of her life drifting in the way you might expect from a Perceiver, Mary was quite motivated and clearly hoped to achieve a well-ordered (if not traditional) life. One example is her marriage to William Godwin, a fellow writer by whom she became pregnant; though she had been pregnant and given birth before, that lover left her. This one, however, promised her that if they married, though it was for the sake of societal decency, he would consider her his equal in every way. Before the marriage, though, Mary actually managed to support herself — by using her God-given literary talents! — at the offices of a new journal that her friend had started. It was a partnership that would last a decade, and Mary continued to show her commitment by writing articles up until her death.

# 13. Lady Gaga

Her Introvert Advantage: Though Lady Gaga is today the "Mother Monster" to millions of fans all around the world, as a youngster, she was just as inconspicuous as the rest of us, albeit with an obvious gift for music. Her descriptions of her childhood are quite normal, but like the Introvert that she is, there were always parts of her life that she kept separate from school friends and that separated her from them. Her intense passion for music meant that she would have to spend hours on her own practicing both piano and voice, and she even enrolled in acting classes. While there are a great many children in the world who participate in extracurriculars like band and choir, Lady Gaga knew from a young age that she both wanted and needed music on a different plane than most other people.

Her Intuitive Advantage: Lady Gaga's Intuitive aspect has helped her carve out a career in a number of ways. First, Intuitives are known for their creativity and their ability to understand and interpret the abstract. For some, that is language, but it can often manifest itself in music, both performing and writing — and Lady Gaga does both. Second, despite her glorious vocal talents, Lady Gaga has made a name for herself by shocking the heck out of everyone with her wild outfits and challenging music videos. Never one to blend in or do what everyone else is doing, Lady Gaga's extraordinarily imaginative mind has collaborated with other artistic sorts to create some of the most powerful and jaw-dropping images out there, whether it's photos of her walking a red carpet in a meat dress, or her depiction of Jesus and Judas as members of a biker gang.

Her Feeling Advantage: Early on in her career, Lady Gaga established herself as a voice for the "weird." There is an epidemic of bullying, where children are taking their own lives because they are picked on or perceive themselves as not "fitting in." Lady Gaga has always been outspoken in her appeal to everyone who feels marginalized, ignored, or even ostracized, and her message is one of compassion and empathy. She has reached out to the world and used her incredible influence to let people of all ages, races, sizes, shapes, orientations, etc. know that they don't have to change for anyone — they are the way they are because that is how they should be. Gaga has also helped to raise millions for different causes, such as disaster relief (particularly in Haiti and Japan) and HIV/AIDS research.

Her Judging Advantage: While Gaga might seem like she's a little bit off-kilter, don't let the stage presence fool you. This is one motivated, disciplined, and tough woman, and she has worked hard for her success. As mentioned, when she was just a child, not even a teenager, her ambitions were well defined, and she was taking classes that would stand her in good stead as an adult — dancing, singing, and acting. While her Intuitive idealism might have dreamed of making it big and changing the very genre of pop music, her Judging aspect is what put those dreams into reality, and she has continued to challenge herself and show her range, from a collaboration with Tony Bennett to singing the "The Hills are Alive" at the 2015 Oscars to great acclaim. Whatever Gaga is doing, she is making it look effortless. But the fact is that this Judging personality is a perfectionist who wants to get it right, down to the tiniest detail.

www.ingramcontent.com/pod-product-compliance
Lightning Source LLC
Chambersburg PA
CBHW070935290526
45795CB00003B/1027